First published in Great Britain by KandyCares.

Copyright ©2016 by Kandy Dolor

All rights reserved. No part of this publication may be reproduced, distributed, or transmitted in any form or by any means, including photocopying, recording, or other electronic or mechanical methods without the prior written permission of the publisher, except in the case of brief quotations embodied in critical reviews and certain other non-commercial uses permitted by copyright law.

A catalogue record for this book is available from the British library.

ISBN 978-0-9934787-1-0

Bored Single
Self-Help For Lonely Single Mothers

By Kandy Dolor

Bored Single

Dedicated To All The Single Mothers Who Are Looking For Real Love.

Contents

Chapter 1- page 9
Single Mother Boredom

Chapter 2- page 17
Don't Waste Time Out Of Boredom With The Wrong One

Chapter 3- page 28
Don't Waste Your Time On A Man Who Isn't Yours

Chapter 4- page 41
Choosing To Stay Single

Chapter 5- page 48
The Highs & Lows Of A Single Mother

Chapter 6- page 57
All types- Of Issues With The Ex

Chapter 7- page 67
New Friendships And Relationships

Chapter 8- page 77
Knowing When To Leave A Toxic Friendship or Relationship

Chapter 9- page 96
Resisting Temptation

Bored Single

Introduction

This self-help book is for single mothers who would like to 'get their life together'. Are you lonely? Angry with your child's father for leaving? Are you in a toxic unhealthy relationship with a casual fling or a so called friend? Looking for love in the wrong places? Have a habit of falling in what you think is love too quickly? Do you know what qualities you are looking for in a partner? Are you really ready for a relationship? Need to cut ties with negative people and situations in your life? Are you scared to move on due to past relationship dramas and failures, trust issues? Don't believe you deserve better? Are you making mistakes out of being bored single? This self-help book gives guidance for single mothers on moving onto new healthy relationships with men after breaking up with the father of their child. Covering many awkward and uncomfortable but real life situations that many women find themselves in such as; seeing married men (or a man who has a partner) still sleeping with your child's father while knowing he is in a relationship with someone else, seeing a man who won't commit to you and many more unfortunate situations that single mothers can find themselves in when feeling lonely, vulnerable and unappreciated.

Relationships with friends are equally important, they say the five people you are around most you eventually turn into. Do you have friends who are positive influences in your life, real friends who support you and you have never had to question their intentions? Do you have friends who are toxic and you know it but still have them around?

Being single is the time to eliminate all the negativity around you, and prepare to plan

Bored Single

how to get what you really want. While setting a positive example for your children.

Only boring women get bored single..

Chapter 1
Single Mother Boredom

No woman in her right mind wants to end up raising children by herself, but unfortunately it does happen. At first the woman may become so busy as a new single mum and throw herself into the daily chores of a mother, cleaning, cooking, washing, etc. But as time passes, she realises she feels lonely, and as though something is missing; and she puts it down to male company. Once the kids are in bed, it's like "what do I do now"..
Some women don't really want to be in a relationship, they simply feel a bit bored and lack a social life or friends.

These women should really be working on themselves, finding things that interest them and that take them out of their comfort zone before entering into a relationship. A lot of women who are raising children alone of the think about their children's fathers and

Bored Single

waste time feeling anger and resentment towards these men for either not supporting their children and the mother of their child as they should, or for having no involvement altogether. Unfortunately, there is nothing you can do to change the situation. It is what it is, I know it is hard, especially if your ex is playing daddy to another woman's child but does nothing for his own or if he is the type that finds himself in a night club every weekend but can't ever seem to find his way to visit his child. I understand how much it hurts if the father of your child doesn't seem to care, love or even know them, but how long will you spend thinking this situation over? It can be easy to fall back into being angry with your situation as a single mother, all it takes is for your child to mention all their friends fathers are in their lives, or attending a school assembly, parents evening, graduation where you can't help but notice all the married parents and you

Bored Single

feel like they see you alone on every occasion so they know your child's father is absent and know that you made a mistake in who you chose to be the father of your child. Plenty of relationships fail, so don't be to hard on yourself or think too much about how others may think about your situation.

Being a single mother does get lonely, and there will be times when you will crave a bit of male attention, miss the physical affection and adult conversation. There will be times when you feel as if you are the only woman you know who doesn't have a man to talk to, laugh with, ask for help with your car, building a wardrobe etc. It might make you feel frustrated and even want to give up on the idea of there being someone out there for you. You wonder if there is something wrong with you, are you too picky, too talkative, too ugly? Are you going to the wrong places? Do you stay home too much? Do you go out too much and still find that nobody is of any interests to you. Do you have thoughts like; Why cant I find love? Don't I deserve to feel loved? Why cant I be OK with being single for the time being? Am i too desperate for that?

Self-hatred can turn anything ghastly.

Do you resort to joining dating websites hoping to meet the one, yet still feeling on the other hand you don't want to waste your time on an online dating culture that mostly serves men who are looking for quick sex. A lot of women are happier when they give up looking for love, the reason for this is they have cut off the longing that was driving them crazy, and commit to taking care of themselves instead of entertaining their belief that only a man can do this for them. If you do meet with any men you have met online then please think of your children when contemplating to begin relations with someone you do not know. It is sad these days how many young women will do things with and for men out of wanting to feel loved, which they later regret when they realise the people that love them the most are right in front of them, their families of course.

It is perfectly normal and understandable to want someone to hold at night. You most probably wake up, get yourself ready and may have to get your child ready too, sort out breakfast, drop the children to nursery or school, go to work or come back home to tidy up and make dinner and by the time you turn around it's time to collect the kids again. Then you just keep going until bedtime doing homework, washing dishes and so on.

If you have no support at all from your children's father then you are on your own with the work load which is enough to make any woman feel vulnerable as to who cares about her, but you have got to be cautious and sensible in your decisions when choosing to bring a man into your life, especially your children's lives. Some women feel that their children don't have a right to dictate or decide in their happiness and must simply accept their new partners. I can not express how important it is that a child's feelings are not left overlooked or ignored when bringing someone new into their lives, this is not something you can just drop on them, it must be introduced and eased in with time and patience. This new man may not be around in the next five years, but your children will, and you want them to have respect for you, not see you as a mother whose priority is seeking love from different men. Before looking for a partner you need to know what it is that makes you think you want or need him, identify why you want a man, will he be filling a gap or a void? In every relationship you need to make out if that person is really capable of making you and your children happy. What are you looking for in him, his qualities, his mannerisms, etc. Always get to know someone first before pushing for a relationship or forcing yourself and your children as a package deal on him, but of course make sure you let him know they are your number one priority in your life. You should wait at least a year before introducing a new partner to your children, in the meantime get to know him. Go out on dates together and see if you are both compatible and have chemistry, if you don't seem like a match then the package deal is irrelevant. If a man is truly interested in you he will welcome and embrace you and your children as a package.

It is okay to be alone; you don't need a man around to be happy. You first have to be whole with just you and your children to get the man that is right for you all. I once heard someone say nonsense about a woman becoming too independent that she was now hard to love, which I think is just stupid

Bored Single

as most men love an independent woman who doesn't need him to good shopping with her or bother him with the majority of petty things other women need to get there mans opinion or attention on things he really isn't interested in. He isn't worried that every month she will ask him for money. He knows she is not the type of woman to ever risk the roof over her children's heads or put faith in a man being able to pay for her to live.

Chapter 2

Don't Waste Time Out Of Boredom With The Wrong One..

When a man you are casually seeing does not want to take things further or begin a relationship it is all you can think about, once a woman has been seeing a man for a while, it is normal for her to be the one who wants things to progress into a committed relationship. It is an annoying, frustrating situation to be in when you love someone and want to build a future with them. Even if you have tried to understand his reasons for not wanting to settle down such as not being ready, does it mean that you have to wait until he is ready? What if that day doesn't come? If you are seeing a man who is unwilling to acknowledge you as his girlfriend and has made it clear that he does not want a relationship with you, do not hold on to hope that he will one day come to realise that you are the one for him; because it probably won't happen.

It is sad how women are willing to lower their standards to be used by a man who does not want anything other from her than her body, a woman who allows and accepts a man telling her that he does not want a relationship, yet still wants to have sex with her, will never be truly respected by that man. Some women are still waiting for a man to call her his girlfriend or commit to her after years of doing everything that couples do together, the woman gives him the best of herself, all her time, her love, her body, she cooks for him, washes his clothes, takes out goods for him on credit in her name, loans him money, buys him gifts, introduces him to her family, even allows

Bored Single

him to move in and still he claims he is single and free to come, go, and do as he pleases, including sleep with who he wants and have no questions asked. The woman may believe that by doing nice things for him and by helping him financially he may start to see her as more than just 'friends' and start to develop stronger feelings towards her, the opposite is true, she is actually giving the man even more reason not to want her as his girlfriend as she is already playing that role and he doesn't have to put in any effort he just takes all she has to give and more, before she knows it the woman is being used and can not even see it because it was all her idea in the first place to give away all her power. Even though the woman has decided to take it upon herself to do these nice things, sooner or later the man starts to have an 'expectation' that she will maintain doing these things without him having to

Bored Single

make her his girlfriend, he may even comfortably make demands;

"Where's the dinner?"

"Didn't I tell you I wanted roast potatoes today"

"Make sure you pay the phone bill"

"wash and iron my dark clothes by Sunday"

That's where the disrespect comes in, the man will have formed a great deal of lack of respect for this woman who is trying so hard to get him to commit himself to her, not only will he sense and see the signs of the woman's desperation to be his number one but he will also eventually become put off by her attempts and the fact she is allowing herself to be treated like this, he will know that she doesn't love, and respect herself or see herself worthy of seeking someone else who will commit to her, so why should he? Most young women fail to realise that they

Bored Single

are responsible for how they allow themselves to be treated, they believe if they keep dressing sexy, keep cooking the finest meals, and keep buying him name brand trainers and expensive gifts that they will succeed in winning his heart, when all that really ends up happening years down the line you regret the day you ever stooped so low and fell for such a mean, selfish, immature man who has no regard or respect for women.

Do not ever loose sight of any dreams you had of yourself getting married, being in a committed relationship, or having a family. Don't push anything that you have wanted for your life aside because of one man who doesn't want a relationship with you, there is a man out there who will.

Bored Single

Don't end up regretting the time you wasted trying to get the attention and commitment from a man who does not and never did deserve it. Maybe you will begin to feel that things are not right for yourself it might be triggered by a comment he made or something he did but the day will cone when deep down you know this is not the type of 'thing' for you, and want more for yourself, but you find it hard to leave because of the amount of time you've spent together and been so close and familiar over the years.

What you have to understand and cone to terms with is that none of it was real, certainty not on his part. It was not a relationship, it wasn't even a friendship, you either were or still are being used. A lot of men try to dismiss women who question their intentions of the future with weak lines like

"You know I got love for you"

Bored Single

"Any thing can happen"

"Never say never"

And they get your hopes up.

You fixate on what he said all day, the fact he said 'never say never' and you take that and start running away with it in your mind with all the possibilities that 'never say never' could lead to and you allow a sentence so meaningless in relation to commitment- to make you happy.

Is that all your happiness is worth at this point? The real question is why are you putting up with this treatment? Is it out of fear of being alone? Is it because the sex is good? Are you trying to fill a void from your father being absent as you were growing up? Did your mother have similar relationship?

Have you discussed what will happen if you fall pregnant? If he doesn't want the responsibility of a relationship will he want the responsibility of a baby?

The last situation you want to find yourself in is being abandoned pregnant, but if it's too late and you are pregnant or if you do get pregnant and he leaves KandyCares has a self-help book called Abandoned Pregnant which is a self help guide for women who are going through pregnancy alone.

It supports; encourages and motivates women who are facing pregnancy and motherhood alone when the father of her child does not want the baby she is carrying.

Some single men who do not want to commit to a woman they are casually seeing will try to make an effort to keep the woman dangling and believing she is making progress with dumb things like buying the woman a ring for her little finger or a friendship ring simply 'marking his territory' which is pretty immature and is messing with this woman's feelings even more. He does not want to commit, but he does not want anyone else to have her either. Control is not love, and lack of commitment is not love either, love is responsible, freely choosing to give and freely choosing to receive.

There are some women who are engaged yet their fiancés will not commit to marriage and they end up wasting years of their lives being cheated on and given excuses as to why the wedding hasn't happened yet like;

"Soon"

"It's not broke why fix it"

"It's money!"

And although these women complain and make threats of it being over they still stay to be treated like doormats. What they don't realise is, if he won't commit to marrying them then he isn't really their fiancé.

Bored Single

Men reveal their efforts, unfortunately their words don't mean a thing.

No woman should have to chase a man to become her husband, that is just asking for a failed marriage.

As hard as it will be you will be much better off and happier with someone who has the same desires and wants similar things as you. Let go and move forward with someone who truly wants the same thing as you. Sadly, another a reason why he won't commit is because he does not see you as wife material. You could be courageous and ask him if he sees you in his future, or if he is open to commitment as time goes by, but it is foolish to believe that you can get him to change his mind and commit to you. You have got to do what is best for you, no matter how attracted you are to him, or how great the sex is or how compatible you may seem to be, if his commitment plans are not compatible with yours then it would be in

Bored Single

your best interests to end the relationship now.

Make a conscious choice for yourself with the awareness of the future you want for yourself in mind. Walk away and do not look back, if he follows and wants to be with you then he will commit, but if he doesn't then he wasn't serious about having you in his life and you had a lucky escape.

Chapter 3

Don't Waste Time On A Man Who Isn't Yours!

The worst thing you could ever do when single is see a man who is already spoken for and expect him to leave his wife or partner for you, or hope it will remain an undercover secret affair. The cycle of a love affair always ends in hurt, wasted time, tears, and broken hearts. What is kept in the dark always comes to light, and even if a man does leave his woman to be with you, who even says that its going to work out between you both or that he won't leave you for someone else. Despite his reassurance in how much you mean to him don't fool yourself into believing that he will end his relationship

Bored Single

with his wife or long term partner to begin a legit relationship with you.

Do you even know this man? I mean really know him? Do you know his bad habits? His flaws? Do you know why his relationship with his current partner is failing? Are you the reason why? Put yourself in this woman's shoes. Does he have a family with her? Take all of this into account when making plans to take what is not yours because karma has a funny way of coming around when we least expect it. Cheating on his wife shows you how he deals with situations that he doesn't like. Most affairs with men who are in relationships start from all the wrong reasons and come down to never truly feeling a fulfilled bond and commitment to their partner.bIf they have children together then that may well be the only bond they now share.

Bored Single

So many women these days just don't seem to care about if a man has a wife or a partner, they even start to speak badly of her simply because she is the woman this man has chosen to be with and may not leave her for someone he just sees as some fun. Get rid of that low self-esteem and go get your own man, you can do it! Women should unite and stop betraying and hurting each other over men who would nit be able to cheat if all women said no! Being involved with a man who is in a relationship not only lead to your heart being broken, but possibly other members of his family as well, are there children involved? If he does have children then your involvement in his life could be seriously damaging to them if they found out about you. Do not be a part of messing up children's lives, do not respect a man who can put his own selfish needs before his children's happiness. Sleeping with a man knowing full well he is also

Bored Single

sleeping with someone else they are in a relationship with is wrong, and it doesn't make you feel good when you think about it i am sure, especially if its her he goes back to at the end of the night he is building you up emotionally and passionately, but then continuously letting you down when it comes to leaving his wife. Whatever he says he is certainty still sleeping with her, men who are in relationships that cheat enjoy having two or more women, why would he leave his partner when he can have his cake an eat it too? Yes there are men who have left their wives when they believe they have met 'the one'.

But the majority of men, they are not leaving. A man can come up with all sorts of reasons when you are questioning him about why he is cheating on his other half, his wife doesn't respect him, they didn't sleep together, etc, they are just excuses because cheating is never right, no decent person would take part in any of it. After being with a married man some women do go through self-esteem issues where they wonder why they settled for less than they deserve, nobody wants to be involved in something that doesn't grow or make progress.

Hiding a secret affair can be hard work and tiring, it can also attack a woman's confidence and self-esteem, you should be able to be shown off to the world by someone who is proud of you. If it has got to a stage where the woman knows about you, and is fighting for her marriage or relationship, remove yourself from the equation and if the man really loves you he will come to you.

But be warned that the fact you were involved with him while he was in a previous relationship may come back to bite you. If you are in a situation where a man is asking you to wait for him to leave a relationship don't do it!

Bored Single

Do not put days which could turn into weeks, months or even years of your life on hold waiting for him to leave her, especially if he ends up having children. How can you want to be with someone and start a future with them yet they are so disrespectful towards his wife?

During this time you could have moved on to someone new, maybe even have got married and started a family of your own, no man is worth you putting your life on pause for. It is upsetting that many women fall into this trap and their are some women who have spent half their lifetimes being a mans dirty secret, they even have secret children the other woman has yet to find out about.

A man who truly loves you and is serious about being with you will never expect you to wait for him to get out of a relationship, let alone ask as he knows you value, love, and respect yourself too much to ever want to cheat on him or anyone else. Your time is too precious to waste, the years go by so quickly as we become older and a relationship with a married man can go on for a long time and can massively affect your chances i your life's success.

The best thing you can do is stay away from men who are involved with other women; you may not be the only woman he has on the side either, cheaters do not only lie to their wives but also to their mistresses, they will tell you whatever they think you want to hear to get what they want. Don't do things you will later regret and end up disliking yourself for, believe that any man you are meant to be with will not have a wife or partner and put it at the top of your dating list.

The worst feeling is whenever you are with this man you are constantly reminded that he isn't your man. You may even find yourself on occasions staying quiet in the background while he answers a call from his

Bored Single

wife, you may hear the difference in the tone and manner which he speaks to her and how different it is when he speaks to you, he may even tell her nice things and call her his heart, babe and other cute words couples call each other. You may even become angry and ask him not to talk to her in front of you, especially if he expects you to be silent in your own home so he can speak to her without her hearing a woman's voice in the background. It's no fun being compared to another woman and you can expect that to happen when you are seeing a married man if you do something he doesn't like he will be sure to let you know his wife doesn't behave like that which is a cheek within itself because he is cheating on her with you. If you lose his respect its over, although he may have been the one to pursue you and made it hard for you to say no, at some level and at some point in time he will have trouble respecting you for settling for such a flawed relationship.

When you are involved with a man who is in a relationship you will never come first in his life, his wife or partner and family will and that won't ever change.

You probably can not even contact him easily as he is covering up his affair with you so he won't always be able to answer the phone and you may be given time when you are allowed to talk to him or you may not even have his main number. You will never be able to rely on him if this is the case.

If you and a man who is either married or in a relationship both decide to enter a friendship with no strings attached where you both clearly understand the terms you will still end up catching feelings so simply avoid it all together. If you found out the guy you were seeing has a girlfriend you did not know about whether you want to accept it or not you are an accomplice in this mans violation of his vows and betraying his wife's trust.

When women do finally move on from being involved with men who are in relationships, they often regret having wasted all their time in an affair that went nowhere and had no purpose.

If you do get into a relationship with a man who is with someone else you need to go into it fully aware of what you are getting yourself into, it will end badly and it could get very ugly. You will never be a priority in his life, Is that what you believe you deserve? Or would you rather learn the hard way?

When i was 16 i began seeing this guy who was five years old, one early morning while i was actually awake doing a friends hair i got a call from a private number, usually i wouldn't answer a withheld number

Bored Single

especially at that time of night, but something made me pick up that call. There was a woman's voice on the other end of the line and she asked me if i was the girlfriend of then guy i was then seeing. I answered yes I was and asked why, she said she couldn't understand how i was this mans girlfriend. She then said told me that the phone would go quiet but asked if I could i shout hello, when i did, i heard the guy i was seeing answer hello as if he was confused, i then clocked in that i had just woken him up and he was obviously with her. I was glad I had a friend with me right then who i could talk to about it and i vowed to never speak to him again. But when he called me from a different number after i wasn't taking his calls for over six weeks he was very apologetic and had so many excuses for what he had done, with me being sixteen at the time i was very naive and believed i loved him.

Bored Single

He told me that we were basically having an affair and that his girlfriend said she would leave him and move to another country if she found out he cheated on her again and that she was serious so i had better know how to wash his clothes, cook the food he likes, find somewhere for him to sleep and do everything she does for him because if she leaves him he then becomes my responsibility.

I can't believe I ever allowed myself to be put in a second best runner up situation like that, but i did and it lasted several years until it got to a point where she and i even started calling each other telling one another about the things he had done and about the latest girl he was cheating with, it was ridiculous.

They did eventually break up and years later so did we.

I gained nothing and lost everything when I was with him wasting years of my life and

Bored Single

turning into someone I barely recognised. The love and respect I had for myself at that time was next to nothing and I allowed myself to be used by false love. I am far from that teenage girl I once was, and embrace the experience as I now know what not to do as a grown woman and shall not be tempted as I know the consequences well.

Chapter 4
Choosing To Stay Single

This does not mean writing off love forever.

As women we need to find happiness within ourselves, no other person can truly fulfil us. We need to live our lives and focus on ourselves. I love it when a woman loves herself enough to stay single and doesn't even find it a problem. It's great when a woman does not need to commit herself to a man because she already has something better going on with herself, she can count on herself, provide for herself etc.

She embraces her single status and does not care about what others think, she spends time educating herself, pampering herself, achieving her own goals and working towards getting what she wants from her life. She is not desperate for a mans love or his attention and does not go out of her way looking for it, she is content within her own life and surroundings, no area in her life needs validation from a man. Very few women know how to be single and do it well. They are not happy and do not want to be alone. They fear being on their own and look for love wherever they go. By looking outside ourselves, we set ourselves up for disappointment. Yet there are so many benefits and advantages of being single rather than being in an unhealthy relationship that makes you unhappy, being alone can help us to grow and learn about ourselves.

When you're single you tend to focus on your goals and it prompts you to look deep inside yourself and identify then become the person who you want to be. When you are in a relationship your plans always seem to take several seats and you become lazy about developing yourself. Being single gives you time to reflect, time to let go, and time to become open to new opportunities. You get the time to do everything you put off now that you are not putting all your energy into a dead end relationship. Feeling content with being single is a critical step towards preparing to move on to better relationships.

Give thought to what you are looking for before entering new relationships, that way you are more likely to have healthy relationship and end unhealthy ones pronto.

The best women often stay single the longest, they love themselves and hold a high standard and value for themselves that they understand their uniqueness so it is not easy to find a good match for themselves, most of all these women have been through

Bored Single

a lot of bad times in relationships as to why they have probably rebuilt their self- love and know their worth. It is nice to be able to do what you want, when you want without having to check in with anyone. Being in a relationship also means having to deal with someone else's issues or problems and you will have to take on the daily dramas of some of their stuff. Being single you get to have your bed to yourself, you have more money and you can focus on your hobbies.

You avoid a second family for example his mum who may disapprove and have a problem with you or any woman her son introduces to her. You also avoid having him judge your family as sometimes our partners know too much and they aren't shy to get it out there when they are heated. If you are a mother then your children will now hopefully have your full undivided attention. Some women can not bare being single, their relationship status on their Facebook page is always changing, they tell friends and family how they have met 'the one' and 'this is it' for them after only knowing the guy a few months. If the woman has children they are most likely always being introduced to a new man too quickly and end up feeling uncomfortable in their own home. Do not allow this to happen under your roof.

If a woman can not stop seeing men then she should do so outside of her family home and not in front of her children who will lose respect for her. Men come and go but your children will always be your children. Never settle for less than you and your children deserve out of feelings of loneliness, it is possible to feel even more alone when you are in a relationship with the wrong person. Be brave enough to believe that you will meet the right man at the right time, timing is everything, that's why we always seem to find love when we least expect it. One of the

Bored Single

things that I love the most about being single is I don't have anyone snoring next to me at night. I do things at my own pace and work around my children.

Deciding to stay single until finding my knight was the best choice i ever made for myself. I really grew and matured as a person and put all my heart into what really matters to me, my children first and foremost, my passion for writing, helping others and so much more.

I am so busy at the moment and having so much fun achieving my dreams and making a better life for my children and I that a man is the last thing on my mind.

I have early mornings and late nights as it is already and just don't have the time for an un-meaningful or unnecessary relationship either.

Bored Single

However, I do know what i want, and I know what I am looking for in a man but I am also fully aware that I need to get on another level within myself to meet this particular type of man who I desire.

I have accomplished more in my life being single than I ever did in any relationship I was in, it was one of the best decisions I ever made in my life, yes I was lonely at first, but I grew to become comfortable in my own surroundings with my children and have put all my focus and energy into raising them and will not waste any of it to go looking for love from a stranger.

I believe that when the time is right, my Mr right will find me.

I want my children to know they always come first in my life.

Chapter 5

The Highs And Lows Of Being A Single Mother

Every single mothers situation is different, so although you may be able to relate to what a friend or someone you know is going through, you will never truly understand how that person feels. The same goes for yourself, nobody can understand how you feel after a bad day, but talking to others may give you a sense of relief and you might even be able to receive help or positive advice. Every single mother has her bad days, times when she is fed up of hearing the kids argue all the time, having to constantly clean up behind everyone, and moments

Bored Single

where she feels unappreciated. The single mother may start to wonder if her life will be like this forever, it's even worse if she is on benefits as she is at home all day. It is easy to loose focus of any dreams you once had and become comfortable in your surroundings if you are living on welfare, it is also easy to feel trapped in the system and feel like there is no point in even trying to get out of it as you may not be better off financially. But don't ever give up on any dream you have, because you will never know what you could have created from your passion, drive and determination. Don't settle for less than you deserve, you only have one life and you won't get another chance to do it all again at 35-50 when you one day wake up full of regret and anger that you didn't do what you were supposed to. And believe me that day will come. My day came and one day I just couldn't stand myself, I was mad at all the wrong choices and bad decisions I had ever made in my life and I felt like I wasn't meant to be where I was, I was destined to be so much. I was angry I had wasted years of my life back and forth between two men who never really loved me, I was mad at myself for choosing the wrong fathers for my children, I was livid at the lifestyle I had brought my children into-this was not my plan. I was upset that I was living on benefits, I was supposed to have an excellent full time job, I am a Dolor after all, and I come from a family or engineers, lawyers, surgeons, and my mums a TV presenter. I was angry with some of my family members and felt like I deserved some help, a way out. I expect it. I am a completely different person now and understand my family worked hard, stayed focused, and made the right choices in their lives which led to their success.

How could I expect them to stop what they were doing to pay their bills to help me? At

Bored Single

the time I felt I was doing nothing with my life, and had no GCSEs or qualifications to get a good job, and I had minimal support with childcare anyway as everyone in the family had jobs.

I had always wanted to write a book and made attempts at novels but always end up throwing it away because I never thought it was good enough, I know now it was because I wasn't truly really yet.

I will never forget the day, years ago I was in my local job centre appealing a turntable down crisis loan, a lady who worked there wrote my appeal word for word while I spoke slowly and directed her where to put exclamation marks etc.. When I returned to the seating area to wait for decision the security approached me and said "I don't mean to be rude, but I overheard your appeal and I think you have excellent speaking and writing skills, your appeal was the best I ever overheard. Don't let having a

Bored Single

special needs child stop you from putting those skills to good use, use your talent to get your way out of the system." I will never forget his kind compliment. And days when I'm feeling low or like I may as well give up on my writing carer, I think of him.

Some women give the impression to others that they are super mums and can do everything themselves, and hats off to those women who really can, but most of these women although they are single mothers receive support from the father of their child, family members or friends.. There are other women out there who have no choice but to do everything themselves without help from their child's father, parents, family members or friends. They have nobody they can rely on, trust or talk to about how they are feeling, coping, etc. and they continue trying to make the best out their situations. Some mothers can tolerate their children's

Bored Single

behaviour when they are spending a lot of time together through their struggles, where as some mothers who have no doubt been strong for too long can find themselves suffering from depression. If you should ever find yourself feeling like you have hit rock bottom with all the responsibilities it is important you reach out to someone as soon as possible. Don't allow the negativity and stress to build up inside of you until the point you can no longer cope. You would not be the first woman to feel this way, when you are a single mother will a mountain or chores and responsibilities it can feel overwhelming, especially when you feel taken for granted,unloved, or lonely. Believe it or not there are people who will try to make you feel even worse about yourself than you already do when you need support the most, so be careful who you reach out to in your time of need. Friends who make bold statements in general such as " This and that could never happen to me" I'm a better mum than ... Or "my kids look better than hers" anyone who comes off as though they are better than anyone else and have never made a mistake etc are not the people to go to for guidance at all.

The single mothers who are content with their lifestyle and have jobs, routines planned out, chores up to date, family too support them but only now seek a meaningful relationship can still suddenly experience 'life' and can find themselves just as lost as the mother who is not content with her life.

It is not selfish of you to want to have some time to yourself when you are a single mother. It's normal and healthy to take a break from the demands of being a single parent and for you to want to socialise with others and take part in activities that you enjoy. The need or desire to enjoy a break from the children is a perfectly reasonable and understandable one. It's great to have time to rediscover positive things about yourself you'd forgotten or never knew.

Working and raising a child all day, every day, is not a balanced lifestyle and you will begin to look at your role as a single mother with resentment. Needing time out from your children while you enjoy yourself is a good thing and does not reflect poorly on you or indicate that you are unable to cope alone.

If you have friends who are still out partying every weekend whether the are married or single, you may feel as though you are missing out and are the only mother who doesn't have a mother or babysitter on tap who will look after your children at the drop of a hat. You are not alone, but the facts are that the partying stops with the arrival of children. It's sad when a single mother is left with low self-esteem because she is doing one of the amazing incredible jobs ever

Bored Single

possible. One of the main things that single mothers become most conscious about when they are not in a relationship is their bodies. They feel their bodies have not gone back to how they'd liked. If you are one of these women don't just sit there feeling sorry for yourself! There is something you can do about it, it's free, and it's called exercise. You can do it! Exercising can give you an instant boost to your self-esteem and energy levels.

Chapter 6
All Types- Of Issues With The Ex

There are many valid reasons why a single mother could feel angry with her child's father. Maybe he has not played a part in his son or daughters life –ever, or he puts relationships with other women before his children, or is a better father to his other children except the child he has with her. Situations like these are very upsetting for both mother and child. Whether or not the child has explained his or her feelings to their mother, the mother will have more than likely picked up on these issues and may try to raise her concerns with the father who may become ignorant and defensive while coming up with excuses as to why things are the way they are, more than likely even throwing the past in the mothers face. Or he may acknowledge the mothers concerns and try to act on making things better for his child. While most people will try to justify the fact that if a father is in a relationship where he lives with his other children he will no doubt have a stronger bond with them and his partner, that does not mean that he should not make an extra effort for the child who does not live with him, simply because that's the way things are. It is upsetting for a mother when her child feels accepted, rejected, unimportant, and least favourite in their fathers life, and it may even bring up old negative feelings of how her child's father treated her when they were in a relationship.

It is completely understandable for a mother to feel anger when the father of her child is putting a relationship with his partner before

Bored Single

his child, unfortunately this happens often. These types of men think that they can set up happy families with someone new while the relationship with the previous family he has made is in tatters, and the women they are with are aware of how little involvement their partner has with his own child yet still actually believe he would never to the same to theirs if they broke up. It is frustrating when a single mum is doing everything by herself while the father of her child is having more children with other women because he isn't taking on the responsibility for the children he already has with her, it hurts when he has a closer bond with his other children who may be much younger than the child he has with her.

It hurts when a woman has given a man a child that he doesn't care about. While some women are able to push their feelings towards their ex aside and focus on raising their child, most women have a hard time with it. They feel as if their ex is just getting away with dodging his responsibilities as a father and is getting off with treating her like her child means nothing. Another common interference in single parenting these days is the involvement of new partners. Men who think it is ok to introduce their children to every Sandra, Kate and Trish they meet, or think it is ok to take their child for the weekend and when they return home the mother learns Kate bathed, combed ... Hair and tucked her into bed, while daddy was out.

Next thing mummy hears is Kate has told everyone she takes care of her child so she should be grateful as if it wasn't for her your child's father wouldn't bother. As petty and far fetched as it sounds, these things DO happen.

Bored Single

If you are angry with your child's father for any of the above reasons as much as it frustrates you please do what is best for your child when it comes to making any rash decisions. Yes, you deserve to be treated with respect as the child's sole carer and provider, but the child also has a right to have a relationship with the father should they wish. I stress that you must not put up with verbal or physical abuse from your ex, and your child would probably be better off without their father in his or her life.

You do not have to put up with being put down or belittled by your child's father, if he does this often and there is nobody who can help with contact so you don't have to see him then stop contact altogether until you either find a solution or he learns manners. Do not allow any woman your ex gets with to make you feel like a loser, you are the real winner because you know what he is really like and you don't have to put up with what

Bored Single

she does or has ahead of her being with him. Even if you haven't met your exes new partner, once your child says good things about her then you will like her too.

The fact is no matter what the situation (excluding urgent matters of concern of course, i.e. abuse) unless your child was being harmed or ill-treated in any way, if you were in a relationship your approach to the situation would be different and you would probably leave your child to figure out his or her fathers mistakes for themselves as they grow older rather than get involved if the matter didn't affect their well being. Holding on to past current issues or feelings towards your ex partner is not going to help you move on. Although you may no longer be in a relationship with the father of your child,

Bored Single

you will still be living in the past by continuing to enter into any negativity with him.

If the father of your child is single or in a relationship but is still able to sleep with you when he wants then I can tell you who is more than likely going to end up hurt in the long run right now, and that person is you. If the father of your child is unwilling to commit to you but wants to use your body for his pleasure then have the respect for yourself to do the right thing and end all forms of physical and sexual contact. Sleeping with an ex is going to hold you back from moving forwards with your life, and when you finally do decide to move on, it will take longer. So end it today, especially if he has a partner, you are better than than. It's a terrible downgrade when women who were once in a relationship with the father or their child end up being his mistress or

Bored Single

side chick. Don't let this happen to you as it will affect your self-esteem down the line. Keep your self-respect, physical health, emotional sanity and common sense where it belongs; in tact.

If you are seeing someone who always seems to be busy until it's time to get it on then his intentions with you are not good unfortunately. Knowing that you are with the wrong person can bring you closer to being with the right one once you make a decision to do something about your situation. If a guy only contacts you in the night or never stays over that right there is a hardcore sign he is only in it for what you have to offer, and could possibly have a girlfriend you don't know about. If he never invites you anywhere, or introduces you to any of his friends, never talks about his personal life and has little or no interest in yours, doesn't care about your feelings, never talks about a future with you, and all

Bored Single

he talks and thinks about with you is sex, then you are being used. Stop all contact with this man, **NOW!**

Never ignore your gut feeling, even if you think what you suspect may only be a possibility that in itself is a gut feeling that is warning you. Keep your eyes open and assess the issue for what it really is. Don't forget that there is plenty more or wherever this man has come from so you can move on and you don't have to stay with a man who I'll treats or disrespects you as if he is the last man on earth.

If you are bored single waiting for a man who is in prison please think carefully before deciding to do his sentence with him while you are out in the real world. Will he be faithful and grateful to you when he returns? Was your relationship solid before he had to go away? Was he a danger to you and your children? Were you in a violent relationship?

Bored Single

Now is the time to figure out and start planning for a better lifestyle.

Chapter 7
New Friendships & Relationships

You will not be single forever, even if you feel that way now, you simply have not met the right one worth yet who is worth your time.

Before you take things anywhere near a relationship with a man, develop a friendship first. It can be all too easy to fall head over heels in what we believe is love within the space of a few weeks, when really women should be spending this time getting to know a man.

His likes, dislikes, interests, hobbies, friends, surroundings, lifestyle, etc.

I mean, **really** get to know him, see how he reacts when he is angry or upset about something, how he manages challenging situations, his relationships with his family, and the relationship he has with his children.

Bored Single

When dating it is crucial to hold onto the things you strongly believe in that are non-negotiable. Maybe your priorities include finding someone who is the same religion as you or who is financially comfortable or likes travelling etc. Every woman has her own list of attributes she desires in a partner, it could be skin tone, muscle structure, height, or just a certain swag. But these are only what is going on **outside** the man, the attributes he possess within is what **really** counts.

 By all means, find yourself a match, or make a list even, but if you are a parent make sure parenting principles are on the top of your list. A man who meets the criteria of your list is a relationship that is more than likely to last. Don't just take his word for it regarding what he tells you about his life, if something does not make sense, add up, or feel right ask questions and don't be afraid to say if you don't like something or the answer you are given.

Bored Single

Most women make the mistake of sleeping with a man too soon, they become attached and start to develop feelings. Do not make this mistake, while it may be a while since you last got any action in the bedroom department i bet it has also been a while since you last felt like trash for sleeping with someone you should not have or feeling awful about allowing some any guy to just use you. You will have built up your self-esteem, self-love, self-respect, self-worth and have come so far to fall back into the arms of an unhealthy relationship.

Find someone who wants the same things as you do and is serious about wanting to build a future with you. Keep your new relationship to yourself for at least a year before telling everyone about it, especially if you have a track record of introducing different men to family and friends. Single mums hardly give up the dream of finding

Bored Single

love, and making a life with someone. Sometimes everything comes together amazingly without a hiccup and the mother meets a man who embraces her and her children, then they go on to live happily. Sometimes things don't happen like that for every woman and having children can seem to prove a hard task in finding a partner when guys all tell her a similar version of;

"I do love you and I really care about you, you're great, but your children are always around and I just want you to myself"

What should a woman's response to that be?

Telling that jerk where to get off of course!

If you have fallen in love make sure you know what this man is prepared to do about becoming a part of your family before you start dreaming of your future with him. If he has made clear that he does not want children, never has, never will and totally can not stand them then leave now. Getting with a man who has anti children issues will only cause major complications and problems in your relationship with your own children, especially in the long run as they get older. Don't fool yourself into thinking he will become minimally involved in the least because at some point after a long stressful day you will resent him for not helping out, and he will resent the time you are spending with your children. Don't lie to yourself and believe he will eventually change his mind and one day fall in love with your kids because they're good kids. A man who says he doesn't like children wont. Even worse, your children could feel his rejection on a daily basis which isn't a good vibe for them and it will affect your relationship with your children. They will not like him and will be very angry with you for bringing him into their lives.

Bored Single

If you have children and are searching for love and marriage, wait for a man who is able to understand that truly loving you means learning to love and have a relationship with your children too because children are a major part of you, and understandably your number one priority and a huge major part of your life. He has to take into account and accept that being with you means understanding your children will aways be the priority. It means staying involved with the whole family, being faithful, honest, committed, loyal, and trustworthy.

Choosing a life partner is one of the most important decisions you will ever make and you should choose wisely.

Make sure you choose a partner who you can rely on and who will always make time for for, whether it's just to spend with you chilling out, or having a talk about something, you know he will be there to support you. No matter what you may face you know you won't have to face it alone because he will be right beside you to comfort you, and even make you laugh through the tough times. Choose a partner who you feel comfortable enough around to do silly stuff like dancing when nobody is looking. It is important to have things is common when you are looking to find that person you want to spend the rest of your life with, you need common grounds to build your relationship on. Of course you won't agree on everything in life or like every single thing that your partner does or is into, but at the end of the day once you are both able to disagree and still come to a resolution and still have shared values that will help you build your future together, you are on to something good. Communication is vital and key in any relationship, as this is what leads to trust. Definitely look for this attribute in a partner. Patience is another important factor in finding a partner, especially when a woman has children to consider. But bare in mind also that good things can take time to come to the surface.

The communication in my past relationships were awful. I wouldn't know how any of my exes were feeling until they blew up on me in anger. This was not a positive sign of a healthy relationship and I knew that deep down yet I stayed and it ruined need my self-esteem.

A man who embraces your children as an opportunity to have even more love in his life is a man to be taken seriously. Although you may have fallen in love with your partner your children haven't and they will be cautious no matter how wonderful you think your guy is. They will have strong feeling about no longer having all of your attention and time. It falls on the adults to be adults and put the children's needs first for a while, they will need help in making the big and small changes that come with accommodating another person in their home and in their lives.

Don't ever forget about your kids being happy just because you are.

Since making changes in your life you may have lost a few friends but that is ok as there is now more time for you to find new ones. Become friends with people who motivate you to be and do better, people who can see your talents even when you can not. People who have ambition, goals, targets, and are working towards them. Making new friendships can be an amazing thing. It is fun when you instantly click with someone and are getting to know more about them. Make friends with people who are so focused on improving themselves that they have no time for drama at all in any area of their lives. Being a good friend is a two way street and you too also have to have the same qualities in the friend you hope to find.

True friendships are not one sided, both people should benefit from knowing each other. Once you attract friends who are sincere in their desire to bring out the best in you you'll attract even more friends who will be there for you, no matter what. Finding true friends to surround yourself with is very valuable, and you will end up meaning so much more to you them enduring friendships that are unhealthy. Try to make good choices and you'll find yourself alongside lifelong friends who will help you make the most out of your life. Friendships tend to get off to a good start when you just click with that person for whatever reason, if you both live locally and are able to hang out easily, and if you have something in common.

Spending time with someone is the key when becoming friends.

Chapter 8
Knowing When To Leave A Toxic Friendship Or Relationship

Knowing when to leave an unhealthy relationship can be tough, but you have to love yourself enough to do the right thing for

Bored Single

your own happiness and peace of mind, don't end up regretting choices you made that you knew would not benefit your life in any way and result in you being the one ending up hurt. It is hard leaving someone that your caught up in and feel you can not leave no matter how unhealthy the relationship is because you are trapped in a familiar cycle, especially if he knows how to manipulate and control you, he may apologise for anything he has done wrong and swear he will never do it again and because you love him you agree to give it one more chance, which you said the last time.

 It isn't good for either person when one or both are not happy, unsatisfied and unfulfilled, it is much better and healthier to separate and move on to a new relationship that brings you happiness and gives you what you need. An unhealthy relationship can consist of many things, physical and

Bored Single

verbal abuse, cheating, arguing, lies, belittling and so much more that can scorn a woman for life and make her become bitter. Most women have all experienced an unhealthy relationship, maybe you are experiencing it now, but you can't or won't leave and neither will he, but what is happening when we hold onto something that is wrong for us is we waste all our energy into fixing up the broken relationship. There is so many better things we could be doing. If you are in a relationship and feel single it is time to leave, if there is no love, and no trust between the two of you then let it go as there is no point in being with a man who you can not trust especially to be there for you when you need him in tough times. Never stay in an unhealthy relationship waiting for it to get better, if changes are not made then it will not get better, couples who keep breaking up and making up every week should separate as this is no way to live and it is completely draining all the constant arguing, falling out, not speaking, worrying, name calling and then a few hours later all is forgiven.

That's just wrong.

Why would you want to get back together with someone who called you horrible names and said awful things to you?

Even if they said it in anger it's not about them it is about you and setting the example and standard for how you allow others to treat you. Do not make or accept excuses from anybody who insults you intentionally. If you are unhappy in any relationship you are in leave, free yourself from the misery, start making the right decisions that will lead you to ultimate happiness.

The most important warning of all that tells you your relationship is unhealthy is your gut feeling. If you can not express your thoughts, feelings or ideas to a significant other out of fear of belittlement, rejection, criticism and not being supported, then that is a sign of an healthy relationship. If after a while the love and affection he showed you at the beginning totally disappears and he has become a completely different person who you feel you now walk on eggshells around then that is another sign of an unhealthy relationship. If he calls you names such as lazy, stupid, ugly etc that is verbal abuse which many women often seem to confuse as love or even find themselves defending his heartless actions by passing it off as oh he only said that because he was angry, he loves me really.

If a man hits you that is never love, that is a man who has lost control.

Do as I say or act like this or I will leave you is a major sign your relationship is unhealthy.

Unhealthy relationships come in many forms, but once you have identified you are in one there are things you can do to help you leave for good or help you to identify if you are in an unhealthy relationship. You could keep a diary and log down things that have taken place in your relationship and see how often there is an argument etc. After we break up with someone or vice versa we tend to forget why we left and boost the relationship up to what it wasn't, this is the time when a woman is at her greatest risk to going back to their chaotic relationship. Reading over the factual note you wrote in your diary will help you to remember what happened in your relationship, why you left and why you will be better off without him.

Ask yourself, would you want your daughter,or sister to be with a man exactly like him? Do you have a daughter? Is she seeing her mother being ill treated or constantly angry, frustrated and upset? You must realise that this is not setting a good example for her or teaching her anything about relationships are supposed to be, this may become normal to her and she could grow up with the belief that constant arguing in a relationship is ok. If you have someone that you could talk to outside of friends and family like a professional who could help you process and come to terms with the loss of your relationship. You could also fund support online, or at your local community centre there may be a group you could join with members who have experiences in leaving unhealthy relationships. I don't think we should judge partners based on our families and friends opinions but i do believe that we should take them into account.

Change everything that can give you ex any way to draw you back in to him, delete and block him from social media sites,and ask your family and friends to also do so that he can not have access to you through anyone. If you ever need to leave a dangerous relationship and need help there a women's refuges and victims groups with trained staff who will help you get through tough times. Don't ever lose yourself and continue to live your life, break away and be free from any chaotic unhealthy relationship.

I remember when I was unhappy in a unhealthy relationship I was in six years ago, during a moment of frustration I remember screaming to the sky to God saying when will I have the strength to leave him, when will this be over?! At that point i had realised just how much I wanted my ex to disappear from my life and how bad he was for me, but i couldn't leave him, and I was begging God to do something to help me. I had gone through periods of not talking to my ex for a few weeks hoping I could eventually cut him off for good but I always kept going backwards. I even had the support of friends who were eager to see me succeed in getting out. It was very hard for me because

Bored Single

i had known this man since i was 15 and here I was at 25 trying to remove him from my life which he was a big part of but for all the wrong reasons and in all the wrong ways.

It was hard for me because after knowing him so long he became a very bad habit of mine.

About a month after asking God for help I discovered I was pregnant and the father of my child who I had known and been with all those years didn't want anything to do with me, my pregnancy or his own child and left me abandoned.

I was supposed to leave him.. I had been working on it for so long, but I am glad things turned out the way they did because my son is both a blessing and a gift.

We all have friends we know aren't for us, even if we have known them for a long time, but now that you are maturing and making significant changes in your life and personal development then you may come to realise that some these friendships are seriously toxic. You may suddenly feel uncomfortable being in this unhealthy friendship.

Unhealthy friendships can be just as bad as an unhealthy relationship, if you are uncertain about a friends loyalty or true feelings about you then keep them at a distance or not have them in your lives at all. There are women who mostly keep male friends because they find them less bitchy and competitive than their female friends. If you ever have a bad feeling about someone who is supposed to be your friend do not ignore it and stay away from that person, the same goes for if you feel that they could be jealous of you. Women can become envious of other women very easily, it doesn't take much. Don't be afraid to drop fake friends

Bored Single

or to distance yourself from people who you no longer have anything in common with, the best time to do this is while you are single. You shouldn't be keeping score in your friendships but if the only time your friend comes around is when they need favours then they could be more of an opportunist than a friend. Do not continue unhealthy friendships after leaving an unhealthy relationship, completely cut off anything and anyone who is not good for you, makes you feel you as if they are better than you etc. Distance yourself from friends who do not love and respect themselves or who constantly seek and crave the attention of a man all they probably come to you with their men dramas all the time and you don't need that while you are single and focusing on yourself. Do not waste your time trying to put your friend on the same page as you, even if she understands what you are saying she will not stop being man crazy and

Bored Single

respect herself until she experiences her own wake up call, even then she still may not change. It is human nature to want to help friends when you can, but there is a fine line between helping someone and being a co-dependant for someone. If your friend just calls you to talk about how badly things are going in her life all the time, she is draining you with an unhealthy friendship. Has she ever made time to listen to you? It can be annoying when you are single, content and on the right track, have started making better decisions for your life but have friends who are not content and call you to listen to them say the same thing over and over they are bringing down your mental attitude, sometimes just listening to them to enabling them to feel like they can call you with their issues all the time. They say we become like the five people we are around most, so choose who you spend your time with wisely and importantly.

Bored Single

When you are making personal growth your thinking slowly begins to change, you may find you even start questioning some of your friendships, disapproving of their lifestyle and how you were ever once like that person and enjoyed talking to them for hours about everything and nothing. They may also realise that you have changed and decide the new you is boring and trying to be too perfect because they can not yet understand and grasp self-love, and you both may end up drifting away from each other mutually. In good friendships people allow each other to change and grow, but in bad friendships someone feels threatened when one person grows or changes.

Do not be afraid to lose friends and do not be afraid to make new ones who inspire and motivate you. It is better to be alone than to spend time with friends who are destructive to your self-esteem, unhealthy relationships can cause enormous damage to your confidence without you even realising it. Your friend might feel you are turning on them but you know that isn't true, you are making positive changes in your life which they may be aware of if you have shared this information with them and if they are honest with themselves while thinking about how much you have changed they may realise that you will not allow them to weigh you down with unnecessary drama that you have just got rid of in your own life and are not about to use your new freed up space for theirs.

They may even decide to stop telling you things out of fear of being judged or the embarrassment of their actions they no longer feel its something they can share with you, once you may have laughed but the new mature woman in you does not find it funny but degrading. Once you let go of negative friends you will find your attitude changes and becomes more positive which

Bored Single

will attract upbeat people into your life. Stop being around friends often leave you feeling agitated, resentful it angry. Often we fail to take the time to have a good long hard look at the people around us to make sure they aren't holding us back and are supporting us. A so called friend who ridicules you, gossips about you, spreads rumours and can not share in your joy when exceptionally great things happen for you such as getting a new house, job, etc.is no friend at all. Don't worry about dropping friends that are no good and whether or not you will regret your decision to keep it moving without them, in time when you think about it you probably regret not getting them out of your life sooner. By losing the negative you allow something more positive to enter your life. It is hard to break up with friends even if they're unhealthy friendships, sometimes you just don't know how to end it but you have to be strong and believe in yourself.

Bored Single

It doesn't matter if you have been friends since nursery, or they go out with family so you feel you have to continue the friendship out of loyalty. If you decide to become more confident and positive but your friends are stuck in their old patterns you need to move on from the life no longer want, ask yourself why do you keep friends who can not help you to achieve your goals or have any of their own. If friends are bringing you down then it is time to move on, life is too short to be limited by the small thinking people you will find around you. If you're around negative people all the time you will start to think this way too, it will rub off on you. Unhealthy friendships that take a lot of energy are really are not worth it.

An unhealthy friendship is hard to maintain, especially if your words seem to always be taken out of context or your actions questioned or if it's just a friend who needs

Bored Single

constant reassurance and praise to be happy.

It's a horrible feeling when you have to withhold your assertiveness and your thoughts with someone who is supposed to be friend, and if you don't like getting into disagreements with them because of their reaction. If you ask a friend for the occasional favour and they always have an excuse or seem to come up with a reason they can not help that person is not your friend. A Lot of people don't believe in themselves so when they see someone else going for gold they immediately try to tear them down, it sounds silly but it happens. If the people closest to you are the ones giving you a tough time when you are trying to improve your life and grow, then your life will be difficult. Don't allow anyone to roadblock your path to success just because they want to stay the same forever. Everyone around you doesn't have to be a

Bored Single

star, but when the majority of your friends are not focused on self-growth they have no intentions to increase their knowledge or skills and no desire to find success. I want you to think about your friends right now, think back to how they were five years ago and what they were doing, now think about where they are today. Are they in the same place? If they are then something is seriously wrong. Don't be around friends who talk about their boyfriends or ex partners every ten minutes. Seriously. There are indeed women who will talk about there partners all day to anyone who will entertain them by listening, they actually believe people are interested, it is draining for a single woman to listen to on Monday your friend was happy, on Tuesday she was sad because he forgot her birthday, on Wednesday they made up etc. she keeps calling you to keep you up to date each time the situation changes. This is enough to make any single

Bored Single

woman grateful of her status, and put her off finding the right type of man she is looking for in the process by her friends drama from the wrong choices she made in being with her partner.

Then there are women who speak of their exes on and off all day, everyday. Although they are no longer together your friend always seems to have the latest on what her ex has been up to, including in his new relationship. This isn't good for you to entertain one bit, as you are moving forward and your friend is clearly stuck in the past, and not focusing on her own life goals, if they have any.

Chapter 9
Resisting Temptation

We have all been there before at some point in our lives, an ex appears from out of nowhere and tells you everything that you have been longing to hear. Or maybe he comes around at a time when you are vulnerable and miss his company, and you end up having an emotional talk and before you know it you are back in his arms.

It's not uncommon for women to fall pray to the temptation of a man, love and sexual attraction are two separate emotions, the second you have done the deed you will feel empty, once you've done it theres no going back. Having sex with someone can be an exciting thought, but when it comes down to it, sexual satisfaction alone will never give you then fulfilment of a happy relationship. Respect you body and don't intentionally hurt yourself, if you want to resist a mans charms whose intentions are no good then you need to ask yourself if you really respect yourself enough to resist him. Confront the temptation and don't push it to the back of your mind thinking i want some fun and will deal with the guilt later.

Also resist any temptation of starting a new relationship while you are working on yourself. Think about all the things you could actually put your mind to and accomplish without the distraction of men. Think about how much you have been through, you deserve happiness and it is worth waiting for. Going backwards is going to make you feel like a loser.

You deserve to be happy, loved, cared for, respected and appreciated.

Even if you don't have the best past you can still make changes that guarantee a great future. It is never too late no matter how old you are to start loving yourself. You have to love yourself before you can expect a man to love you and the same goes for respect. People will treat you however you allow them to.

Create your own goals and stick to them.

When someone comes into your life they can go along for the ride or get passed by.

Drive your life towards your happiness, your success, and your family values.

In this way, you do not lose yourself in a relationship or when it ends, whether that be with a man or a friend.

Think positively, listening to affirmations that empower women can help boost your confidence.

You will be feeling much happier, positive and drama free once clearing certain people and their negativity out of your life. You may now find that you don't even have time for what you once did, like talking on the phone to friends for hours, watching TV, etc.

You might now decide to use that time doing something more constructive like job searching, working on a goal, etc.

Become the woman you always wanted to be, don't be afraid of what others say or think about you, stay strong and follow your mind. Step outside of your comfort zone, go to new places, meet new people and socialise. Change your appearance, your hair, the way you dress, and simply feel good about yourself.

Bored Single

Be confident enough to venture out to places by yourself.

Do not wait on anyone's approval, validation, or time. You are no longer in denial about who you are or what it is you want from your life. Create a vision board, pin up everything you would like to accomplish in the next ten years, include everything, pictures of yourself and your children, and all the things you are working towards to achieve. It could be anything you wish for, nothing is impossible within reason; once you put in the working continue you can do anything.

It is important that you stay in a positive frame of mind while taking action to improve your life. Do not look back or allow the past to stop you from continuing moving forwards. The same goes for having people around who will stop you from making progress by trying to drag you back into their world. Stay focused and do not lose sight of

Bored Single

what you are trying to achieve for *your* life. If you have children do it for them, set a strong positive example for them and always make sure your children are your number one priority. Even if you feel lonely and start to miss the lifestyle you once lived or those circle of friends who really weren't your friends, don't look back, you aren't missing anything. You probably don't even realise how far you have come. Don't worry about what anyone else is doing and stay focused on your own goals. If you feel lonely one night, don't pick up the phone to seek comfort in a man who only has intentions of using you, stay single and wait to be in the company of a man who genuinely loves and respects you. On that lonely night read a book, watch a movie, talk to a friend, just don't waste any more time making the wrong choices for yourself when it comes to men, don't put yourself in a situation where you end up hurt or worse.

Bored Single

Don't go back to those unhealthy friendships that were weighing you down with drama, even if you miss a particular thing about that person you ended the friendship with, don't go back! Slowly but surely over time people will notice the change in you and may even surprise you by meeting your standards, you may even inspire someone to make changes and better their own lives after witnessing your transition. You could become a positive role model to others and may find people value your opinion a lot more.

No matter what happens in your life always keep pushing forwards.

Making changes can be challenging, especially when someone is used to living a certain lifestyle. But whenever anyone wants to better their lives in any way, change must take place in order to get the desired results, and having patience is key and a must, as things don't happen straight away. It all depends on how committed you are to

Bored Single

accomplishing your goals. hard for me when i first decided to make changes in my life and stick to them. It was easy when it came to having no further interest in men who i knew were wrong for me, but cutting ties with friends who were negative influences was a bit harder. I felt like I didn't want to miss out on anything and become boring, but I realised that those particular people were not going to change, or benefit my life in any way, I was making positive changes and any wasn't prepared to allow anybody into my life who I thought had the potential to drag my life back into chaos. I was not entertaining anyone and any form of drama had to go. I made these positive changes not only for myself, but to set a great example for my children. It has been five years since I actively started making changes in my life, this past year I have grown in many ways. I feel more positive, I motivate myself and believe I can accomplish everything I put my

Bored Single

mind to. I am working really hard at bettering my life. I am happy and I love myself, i don't meed a man to make me feel worthy of living, my kids are enough.

I have been through so many tough times throughout my life which I could have avoided but now I have learnt from those mistakes. I now keep going without a second thought because I know where I want to get to and as I continue to make more and more positive changes the more doors that open for me.

Don't ever feel like any changes you want to make within yourself are a waste of time, and don't ever forget that it is not too late. You are in full control of your life, and how you think. It is hard at first but time you keep telling yourself and truly believing you are making positive changes and you will start to slowly notice that you are making progress and you will feel much happier with your life, more confident and fully in control.

Bored Single

Never stop making changes to better your life, and never and never give anyone the power to stop you or cause you to lose sight of your ultimate target. Don't forget that things do not happen instantly, and we get out whatever we put in. If you are not making an effort then don't expect anything to happen. Things happen, you might have a bad day and find that feelings of loneliness take over because you simply would like to be comforted. Learn how to comfort yourself, whether that be by losing yourself in a good book, exercising, watching TV, or even eating ice cream! Don't sit there feeling sorry for yourself because you have chosen to stay single not because you actually want to, but because you just haven't met your Mr right. Be proud of yourself that you are even doing this, you love yourself that much that you are not prepared for anyone to play with your emotions or your body, you are no toy. You

Bored Single

know your worth, and your not willing to put yourself up for grabs to anyone who is not what you need to build a life with. Don't allow an attractive face or seductive words to backtrack you, stay loyal to yourself and remember why you have chosen to remain single.

Don't stop believing in the love you are hoping for, it will find you if you believe it's out there for you. Whatever your dream, keep pushing for it, even if you lost sight of it for a while or it became out of reach, steal it back. Don't let anything stop you from becoming who it is you have always wanted to be. Nothing changes or happens by itself, it is down to you to create the lifestyle and happiness you want for your self, it will not come easy and sometimes you will lose sight on what you are working towards during the process. If you are serious about wanting better for yourself then no matter how many times you may fall behind, in time you will

Bored Single

have your plan firmly in place and be able to follow it without a hitch. Even if problems arise you will have learnt how to manage your reactions and the situation drama free.

Tips..

- Throw yourself into things that interest you such as new hobbies, and going places you have always wanted to visit. Take yourself outside of your usual comfort zone and explore all this world has to offer.

- Never stop educating yourself- read up on things you have always wondered or wanted to find out about. It could be your families historical background or anything you've always had a desire to do.

- Spend time with your children, get to know them properly and try doing the things with them that your own parents did or never got around to doing with you.

- Start a vision board, choose words and images which inspire you and make you feel good about yourself. Use your vision board to help you achieve your goals and dreams in all areas of your life. You will be amazed at how the images and words that start coming to mind once you set your intentions for what you feel and what you want. Include your children in this activity and encourage them to start their own vision boards that helps them to unlock their dreams. Make the law of attraction work!

- Being single has it's high and low moments, but do not doubt for a second that rolling solo can be way better than dating. Being single may be one of the only times in your life when you are able to do whatever it is you want, whenever you want, and when you want it.. There are limitless activities that single women can engage in that includes excitement!

Appreciate being free!

Go dancing! Dancing is a great and fun way to spend time with friends or meet others.

Take a picnic to the park, bring a book ,or a friend and have a catch up!

Consider joining a gym or fitness club, or even go running in your local park.

Only boring women get bored!

- Never forget that one of the best relationships a woman can ever have is with herself.
- Create strategic plans and write down your goals, include a date you would like to complete these goals by

- because hope alone does not accomplish anything.
- Single women have the best opportunity to develop their knowledge and life experiences.

- You are not alone when you feel lonely, every woman experiences a period of loneliness at some time in their life. Whether they are alone out of choice or circumstance. To truly overcome the loneliness as a single woman you must first learn how to appreciate your own company.

- Consider your attitude towards being alone and change it.

- Start new projects.

- Experiment with new recipes, or explore an area of interest to you.

- Keep your mind engaged so that you experience the feeling of solitude, rather than loneliness.

- Build up a social network, you need to connect with others to thrive emotionally. Attend community gatherings or visit somewhere around your interest. Find classes or clubs which people engage in activities that you enjoy.

- Avoid negative thinking such as;
"I am lonely because I'm ugly"
"My whole life is a flop!"
Instead of bringing yourself down, learn to accept the fact that in this moment in time you are lonely, but

you will not always feel this way, and there are things you can do to change it.

- Learn to be happy with or without a partner. Even in long-term relationships people still experience loneliness.

- It is **your** right and responsibility to create your own happiness.

- Loneliness is one of the most common emotions shared between single mothers. Remember you are not alone, it's not just happening to you.

- Stay busy; take the kids out, swimming, on long nature walks, bowling, museums, clean the house, iron the clothes, etc. keeping busy starves of the loneliness.

- Stay focused on the positives.

- Put your energy into your children, let them know and feel that they are the most important things in your life.

- Throw yourself into being a mummy, but do not forget that you are a woman too. Take a night out for you where you do the whole 'me time' thing. Give yourself a facial, do your nails, moisturise, feel good about yourself!
Join a book club, or a support group for single mums. It helps a lot when you become friends with single parents who are going through the

same thing, because you know you are not the only one having a hard time.

- Work out who can care for your children while you take some time out for yourself. Do you have family, friends or neighbours who you can trust and rely on?

- Allow yourself to grow, dealing with loneliness and overcoming it is a life-changing process that shows your children to have a lot of courage.

- As a single woman you will become stronger and more self-sufficient than you ever were before. You will be able to do almost anything on your own, including build a wardrobe!

- Use this time as a chance to really get to know who you are without any influence from a partner.

- Start a free course! Go online and find something you have always wanted to learn.

- Go to the movies, theatre, functions and plays. Find out where you can get discounted tickets or try saving up for a show you would really like to see.

- Socialise with friends who have children so that you can have the children all play together while the adults have a cup of coffee and a chat.

- Take your children out hiking, on a picnic, etc. going outdoors is energising for you all.

- Go on holiday with your children! The change of environment will benefit you all, you will feel refreshed and there will be a new side to mummy that your children will see and love!

- Be careful if you are meeting someone you met online or who you don't know. Always meet in public and never leave to go anywhere with them until you know them a lot more. Don't let anyone into your home who you don't know well. When you are bringing someone home for the first time you can even have a friend or neighbour drop in 'unexpectedly' (even during a date) just to make sure you're ok.

- You never know where things are going to end up when you are dating someone new so always keep things light but enjoyable too.

- Talk to other single mums online, share your experiences, ideas, tips and more about life as a single mother.

- Collaborate with your children, for example, cook dinner together.

- Find an outlet for yourself that has nothing to do with you being a mother.

- Make the time! Having a social life doesn't happen unless you make it happen!

Bored Single

Signs you are ready to begin a relationship..

- You have a positive attitude when speaking about men
- You have moved on and let go of past experiences where you're heart got broken
- You can no longer tolerate drama
- You are happy being single
- You are ready to mix and blend you're life with someone else's
- You are socialising, and getting yourself out there
- You don't need someone to complete you
- Your ex is no longer an issue or factor in your life

- You have reflected on why past relationships didn't work out

Warning signals..
- He never seen takes you on a date
- He won't introduce you to his family
- He lies or over exaggerates
- He doesn't work or can't keep a job
- He is a hustler
- He switches personas in public
- He doesn't like children
- What he says doesn't match what he does
- He waits until the last moment to commit to any plans you make
- He makes you cry more than he makes you laugh.
- Your personal growth stops flourishing during the relationship
- You feel drained by him

Bored Single

- Constant arguments and conflict
- His love seems to have too much power over you
- Nothing is positive
- Being in need or a being a habit, is confused with being in love
- You feel worse about yourself
- Your focuses are changing towards his needs, wants, issues..
- You begin to lose yourself trying to find him

Things to do for daily self-improvement:

- Meditate
- Eat healthy
- Read everyday
- Manage your time
- Overcome your fears
- Be good to yourself
- Learn more skills
- Write a letter to your future self
- Acknowledge your flaws
- Learn from those who inspire you
- Visualise in your mind everyday how you would like to act and behave. Repeat it several times a day, everyday constantly reminding yourself of the changes you desire to make.
- Quit a bad habit
- Avoid toxic or negative people
- Start a blog

- Get a life coach or a mentor

Bored Single

- Start a 30 day challenge
- Start a business
- Read one inspirational personal development story per day
-
- Learn how to let go of the past
- Get into action!

Bored Single

Do not be be disappointed if you don't attain fast results. No matter how many times you fail you will begin to see your life change once your efforts persevere, never give up on improving yourself! Always remind yourself of your worthiness, feeling worthy, loved, and accepted comes from within. Loving yourself starts with you, take action and begin to create a amazing life for yourself, one step at a time is all it takes to proceed forward. Believe in the limitless opportunities that can become available to you. Do not allow toxic people into your life, learn from your mistakes and keep it moving. Stay focused on the positives in your life. When you start to love yourself your life

Bored Single

really does improve in ways you couldn't imagine!

Write down all the things you would like to achieve while you are single. If you need to use a separate sheet of paper to continue then do so.

Bored Single

Bored Single

Bored Single

Now write down a list of things you have tried to achieve for yourself while being in a relationship, but failed or took a back seat due to distractions.

Bored Single

Bored Single

Write about how you feel when you think of the wasted energy you could have put into improving your life or starting a career on a relationship that didn't last instead

Look back to this whenever a man comes along who you fall head over heels in love with and gets you off track in your goals.. And remember, nothing lasts forever.

Bored Single

Bored Single

Bored Single

Write down the qualities you desire in a man

Bored Single

Bored Single

Now list the qualities you possess

Bored Single

Bored Single

Match the qualities you want in a partner with your own.. Do they seem to be compatible? Do you need to improve any of your own qualities before you can have an 'expectation' from the quality of others?

Bored Single

Bored Single

Write down what you feel you need to work on to attract the type of partner you require.

For example; I always fall for bad boys, however I would now like to date an educated man who is mature. To attract this type of man I could..

Bored Single

Bored Single

Make a list of all your goals, dreams, and ambitions.

Bored Single

Bored Single

Write down a step by step guide as to how you can accomplish your goals.

Do you need further education? A mentor? Whatever it is write it below and then jot down a plan on how you can achieve them, set a realistic date you hope to accomplish your targets and work towards making it happen!

Bored Single

Bored Single

Bored Single

How can you teach, encourage and set a positive example for your children on how to avoid the wrong types of partners and how not to become these types?

Bored Single

Bored Single

How can you set a positive example as a single mother to your children?

Bored Single

Bored Single

Write a letter to your future self using all you have written above, when you are going through challenges that make you feel like you just want to give up, read your letter and remember everything you are working towards building for your children and for yourself.

May you love yourself and attract love in return..

Bored Single

Notes

Bored Single

Notes

Bored Single

Notes

Bored Single

Notes

Bored Single

Notes

Bored Single

Notes

Bored Single

Notes

Bored Single

Notes

About The Author

Kandy Dolor was born in 1985, she developed a passion for writing at seven years old beginning with poems.

Kandy lives with her two children in London and is the founder of KandyCares- Self Help a Books For Women.

Kandy Dolor is available to give author talks about her books and real life experiences, book signings and motivational speeches at all self-help related events and functions.

www.ingramcontent.com/pod-product-compliance
Lightning Source LLC
Chambersburg PA
CBHW071507040426
42444CB00008B/1528